I0485444

COSMIC COLORING

MAGIC MANDALAS

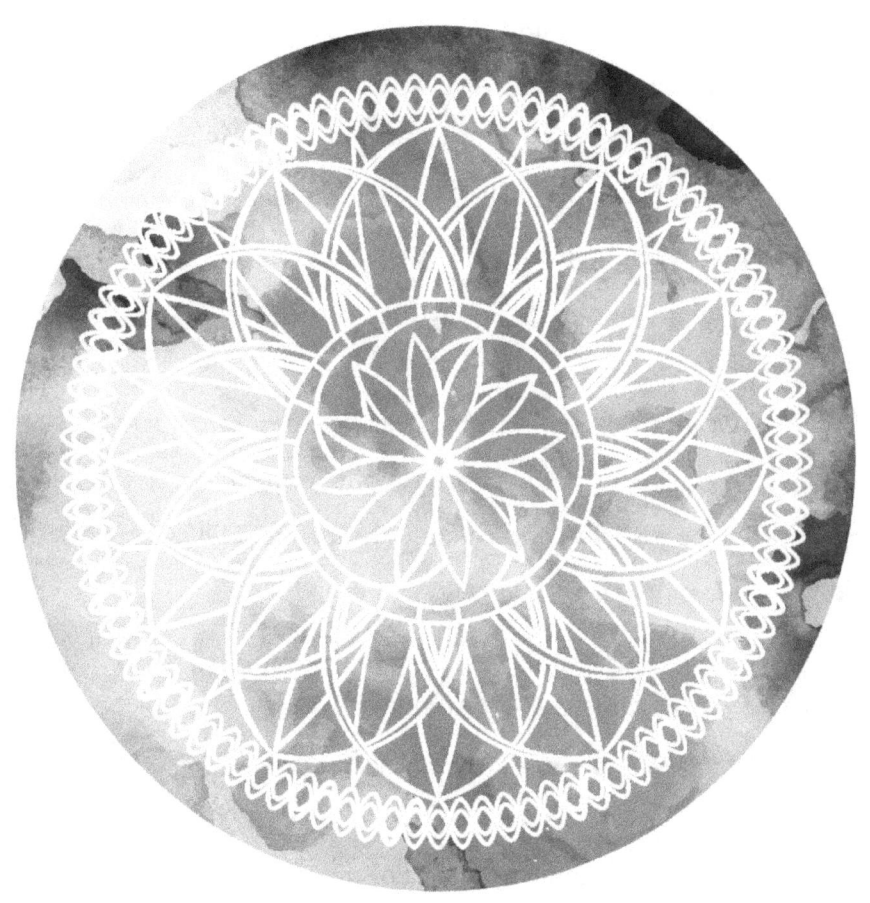

ALAN KIDDLE

SERIES 1

ISBN: 1515366251
ISBN-13: 9781515366256

Welcome!

Thank you for purchasing your book.

By coloring Mandalas, you allow yourself to play. By playing, you open up a range of creative and intuitive processes that we don't always experience in our day-to-day lives.

Creative play opens up our spirits and facilitates a re-connection to ourselves while we are awash with the busy – ness of life.

Let's Stay in Touch

Keep an eye out for more books from me as I create a series of Mandalas designed with you in mind. I will publish announcements for new books on my FaceBook page below and I want to hear from YOU what you would like to see more of.

Join our Facebook group to share your work

https://www.facebook.com/groups/cosmicmandalas/

For feedback, requests, suggestions, questions etc you can email me here: cosmiccoloring@gmail.com

Now, time to go color!

The aim is for you to HAVE FUN !

TIPS & HINTS

Relax, there is no wrong way to do this.

Almost any color combination will look good. You can choose colored pencils,

markers, crayons or pastels or more.

Whichever you choose please be aware that some bleed through might occur with anything other than crayons or pencil so I strongly advise placing a blank sheet behind the page you are coloring to avoid bleeding through the page issues.

You could also copy the pages to keep your book fresh. Just relax, begin and don't worry about the right way to do things. Allow yourself to relax and go for it.

You might enjoy a quiet uninterrupted space with as much natural light as possible, or put on some music you love and lose yourself to the fun and chill out time.

Coloring Mandalas are also highly recommended for:

Therapists

Teachers

Counselors

Stress Relief

Meditation

Anxiety relief

Coloring Partys with Friends

Hand Eye Coordination

Remember, turn off the phones, TV and gift yourself quiet uninterrupted time for your Mandala coloring.

You deserve it!

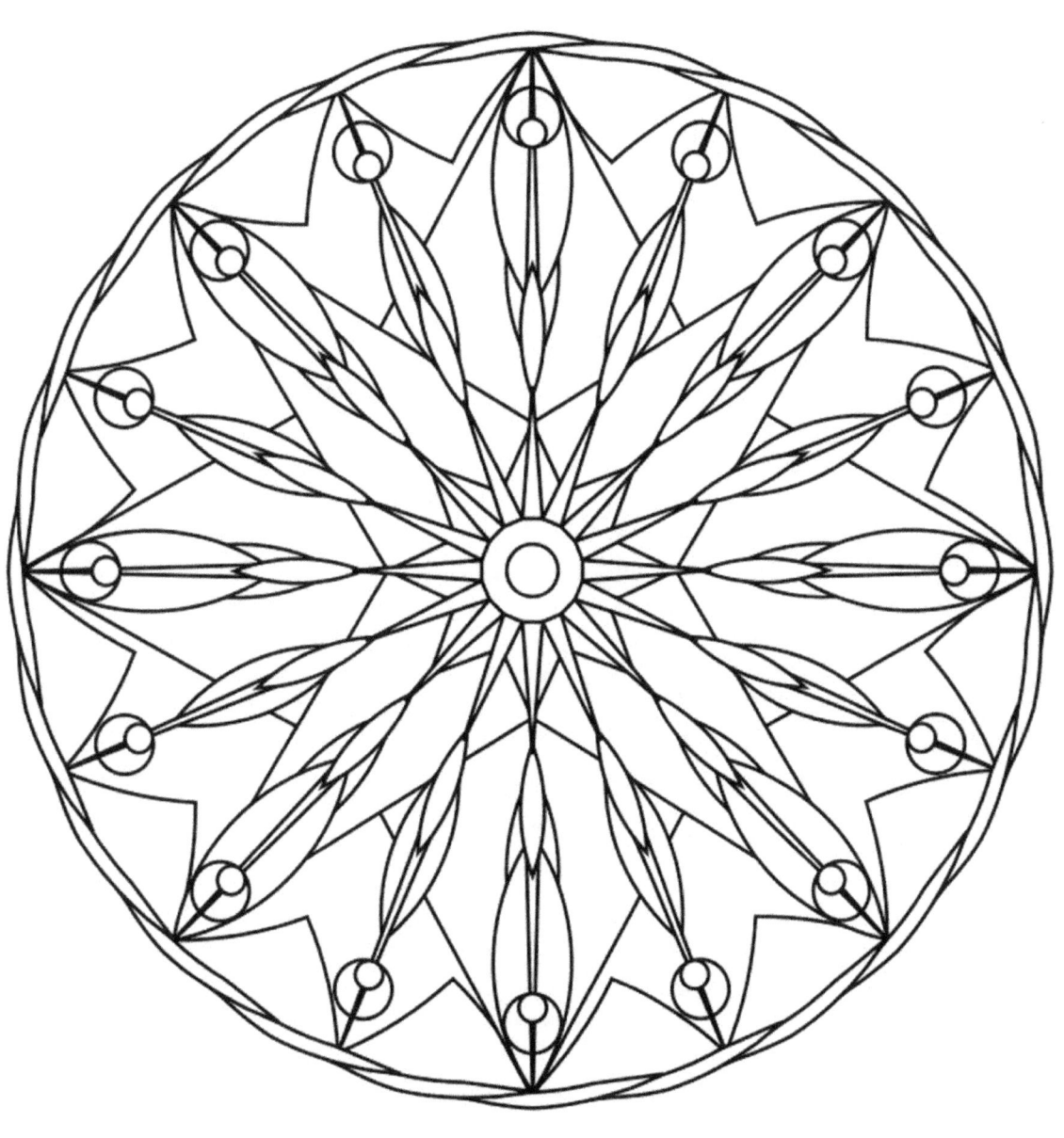

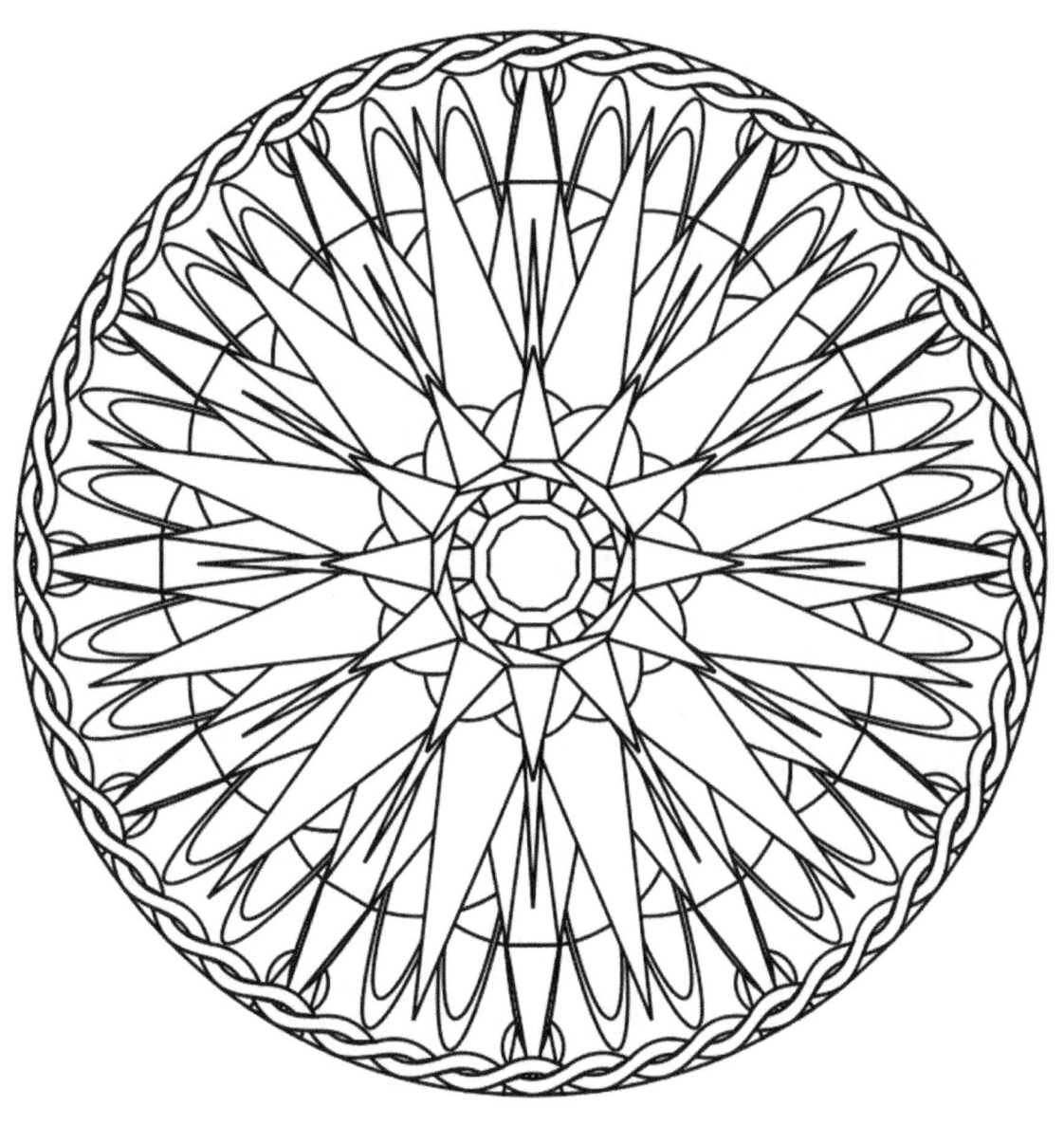

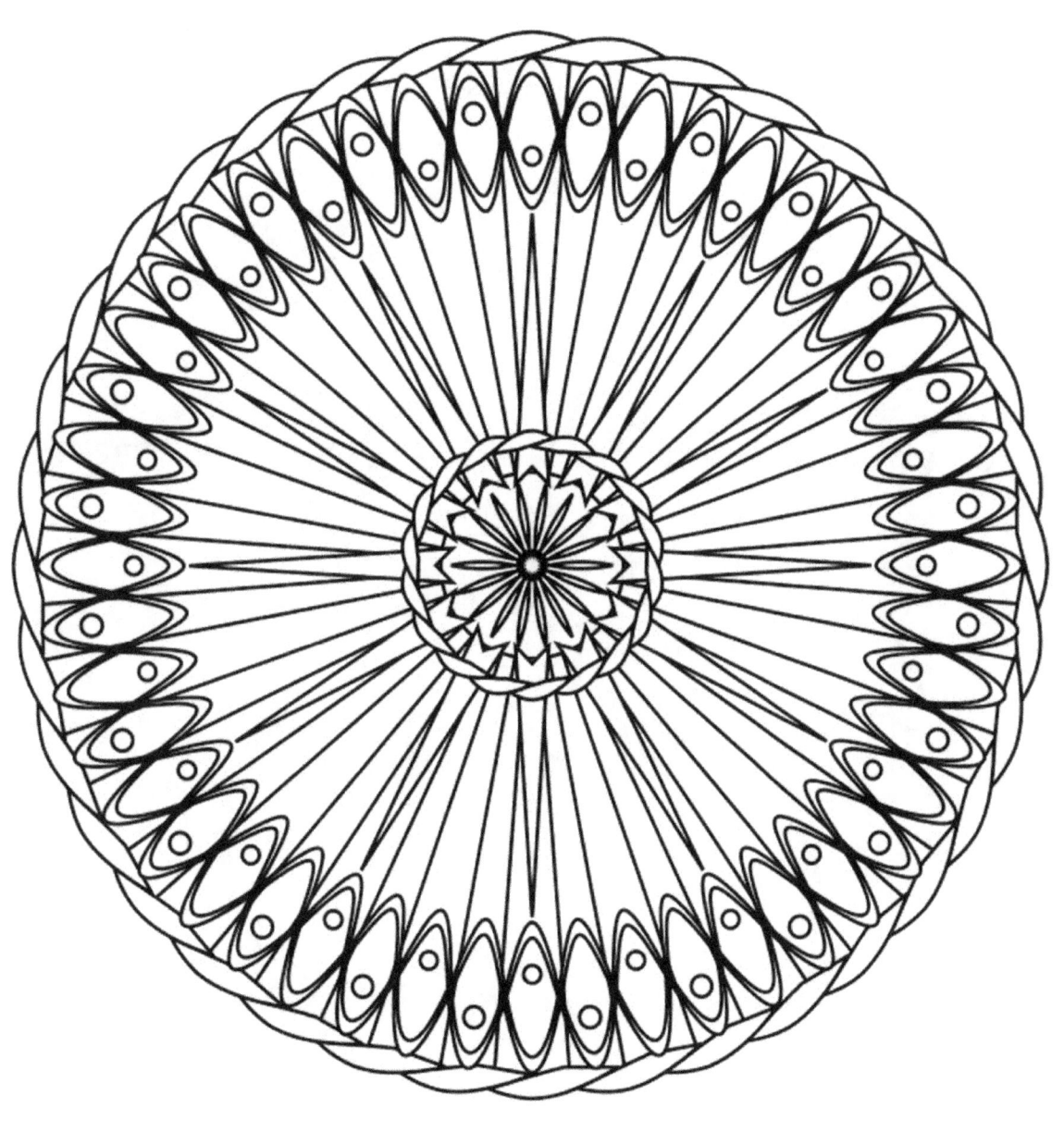

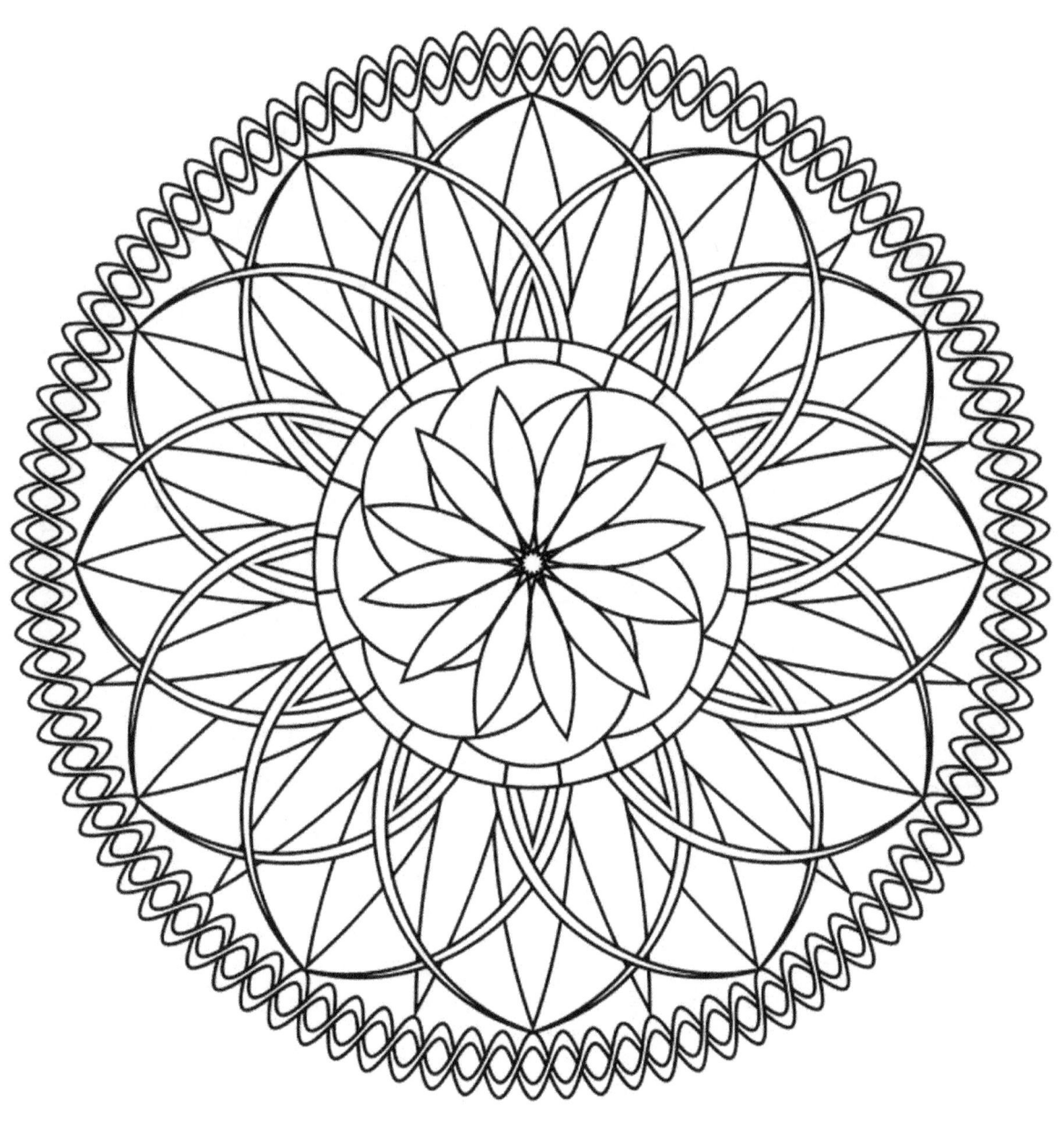

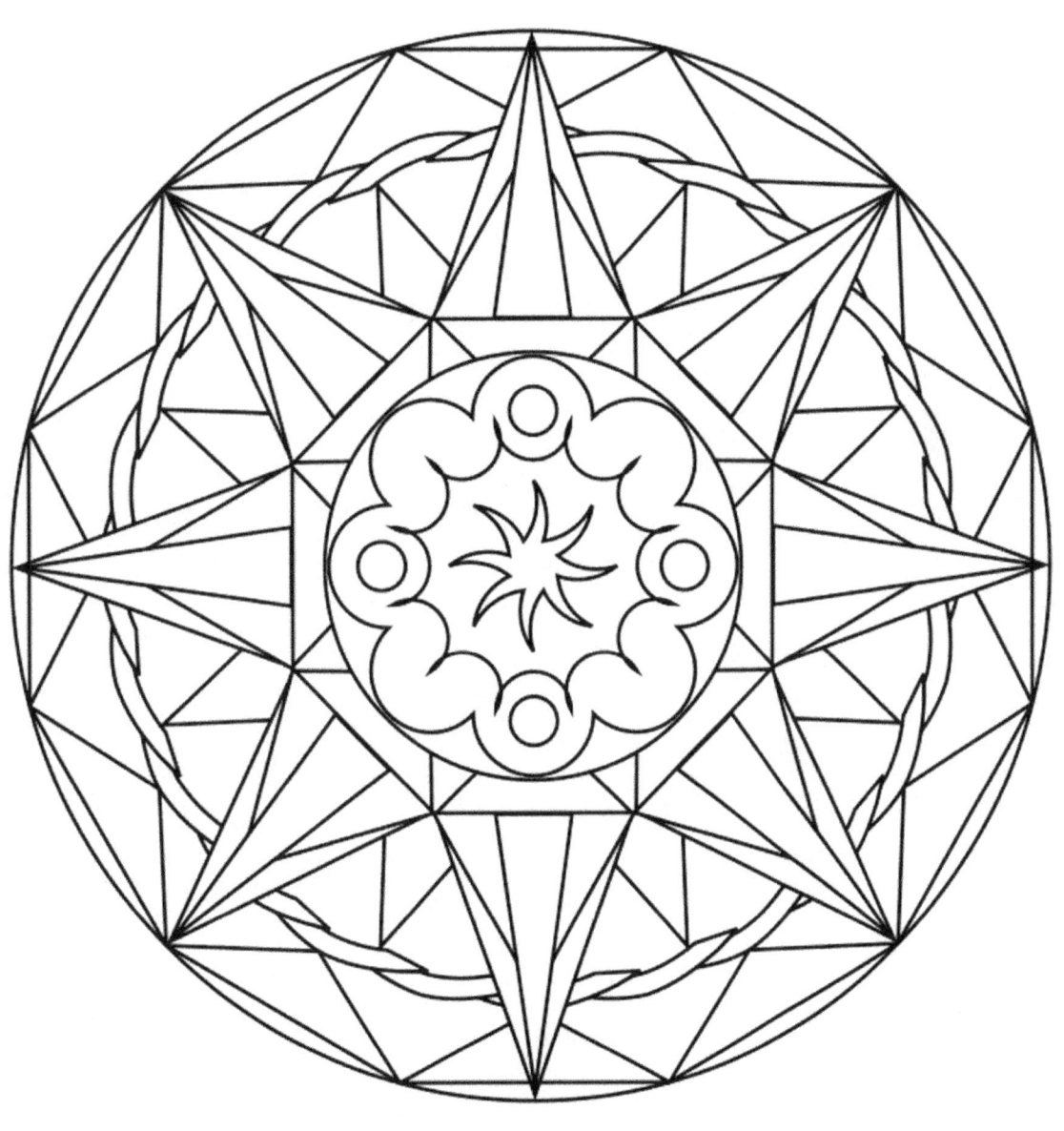

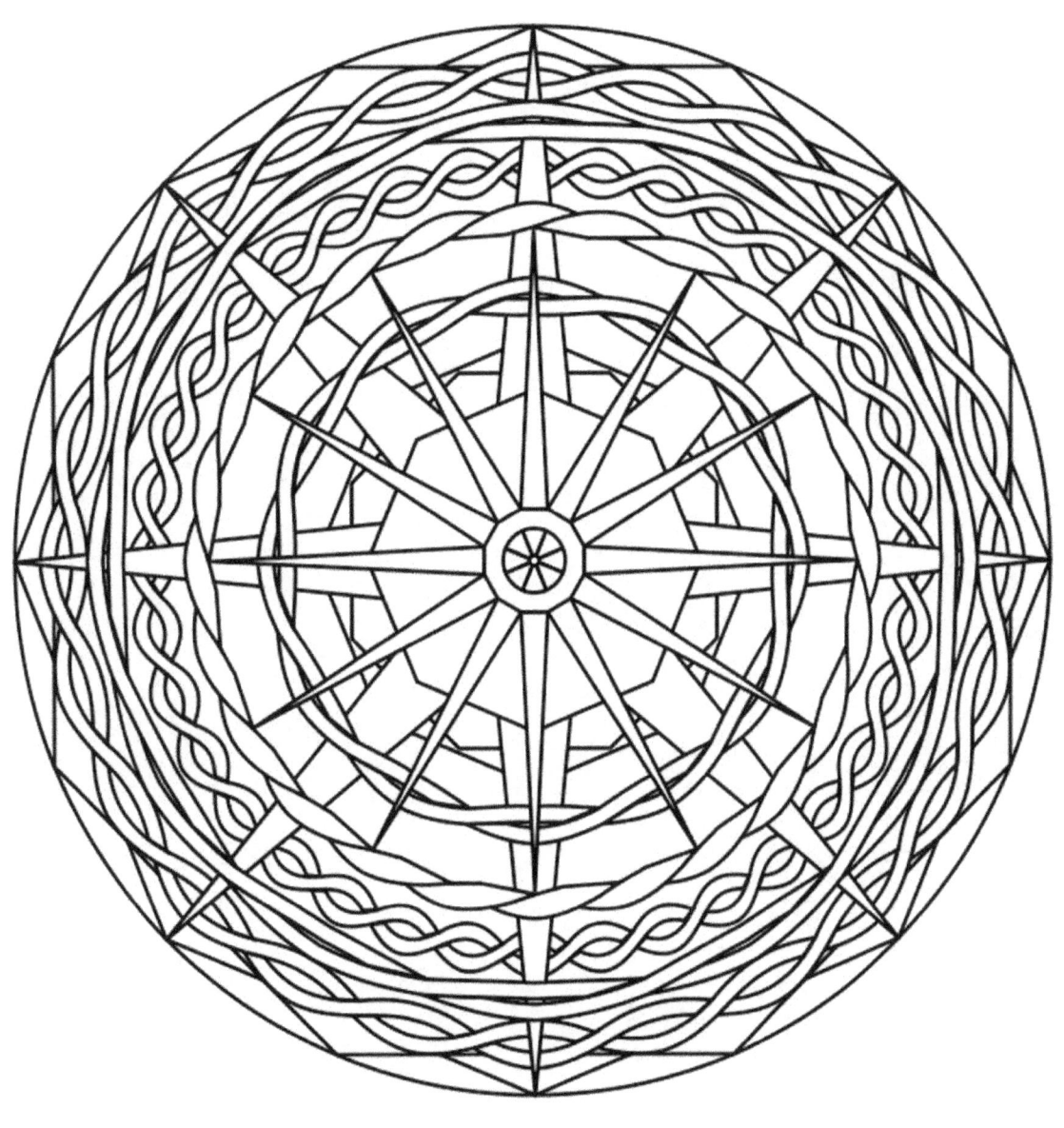

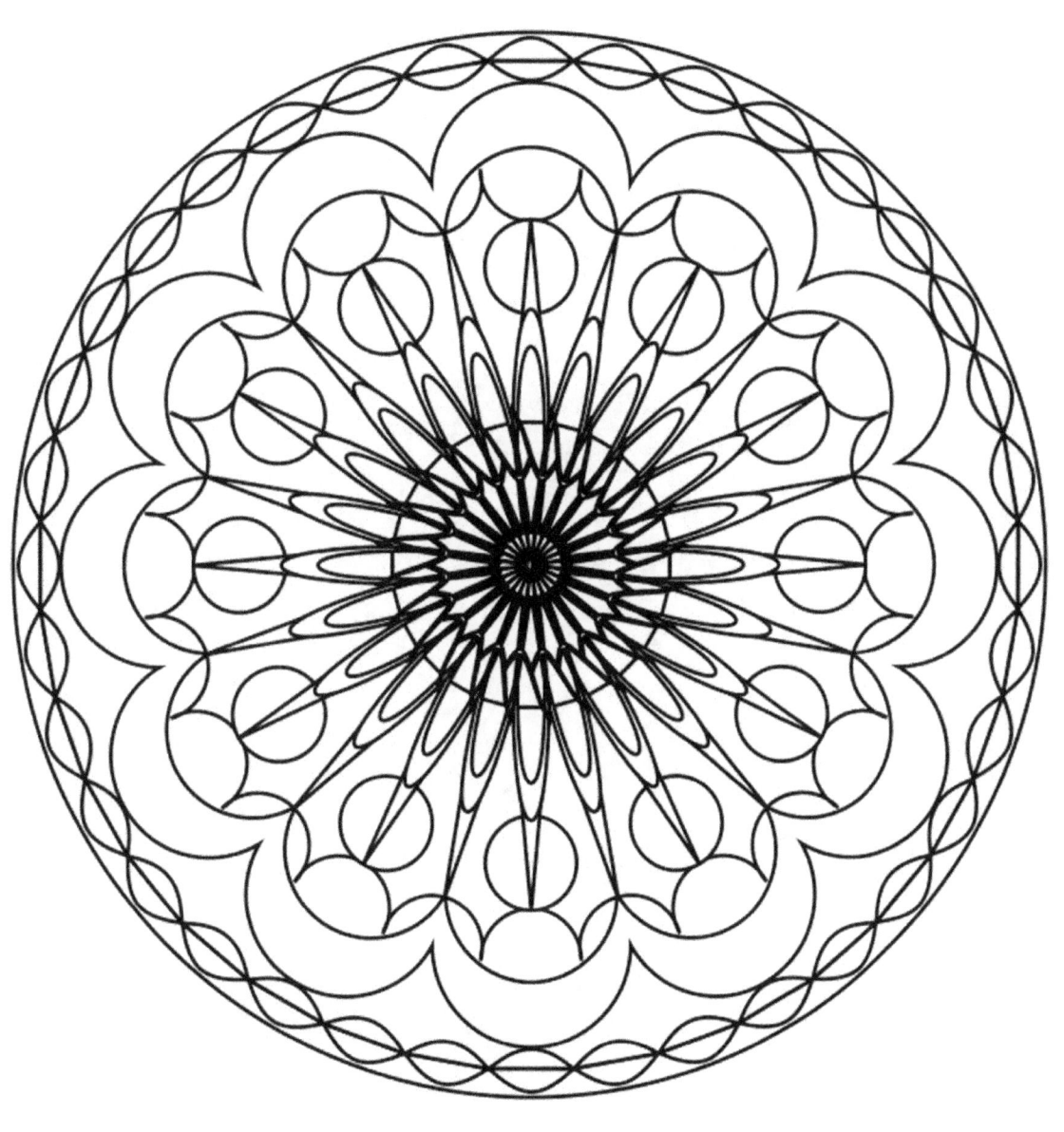

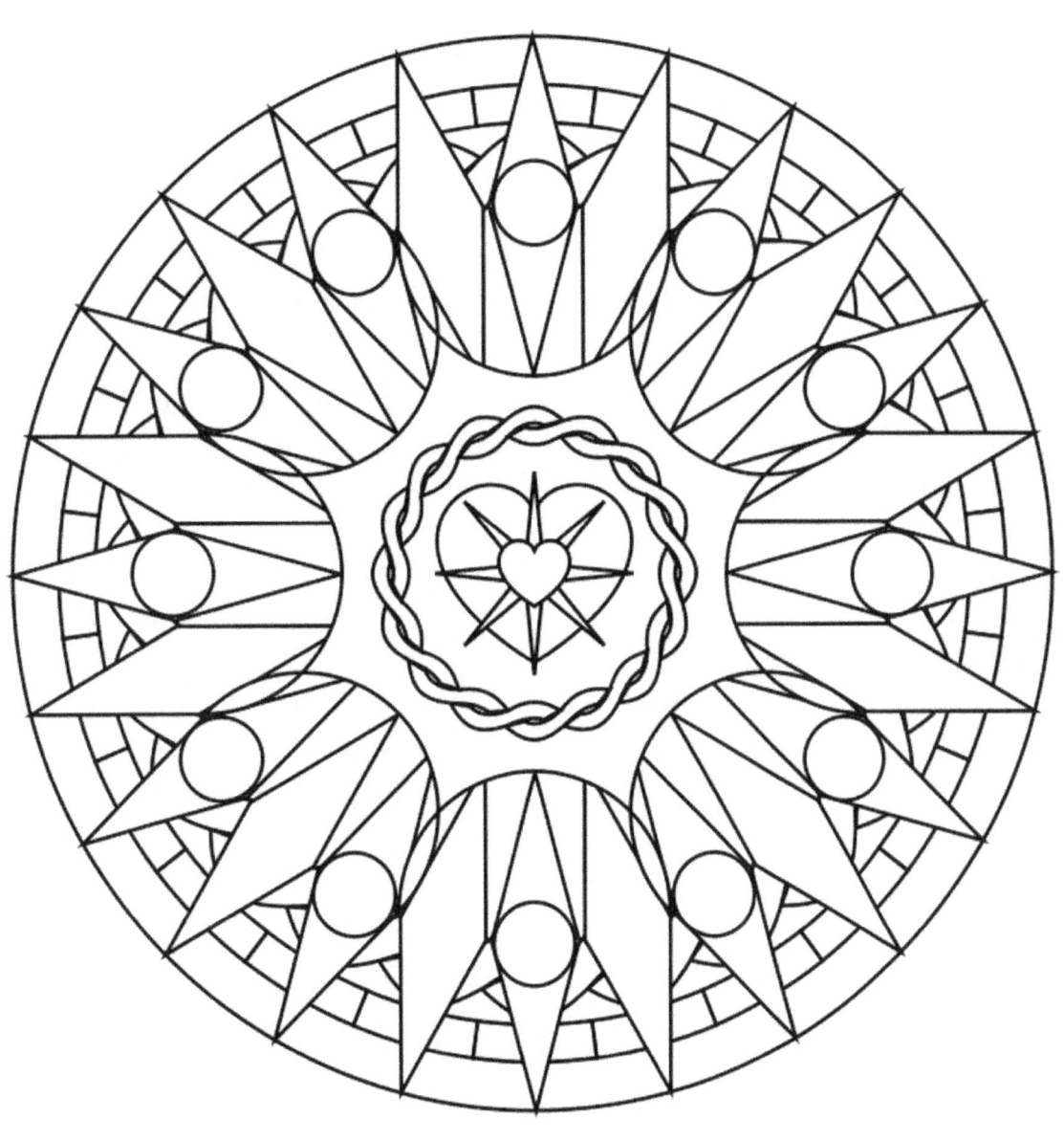

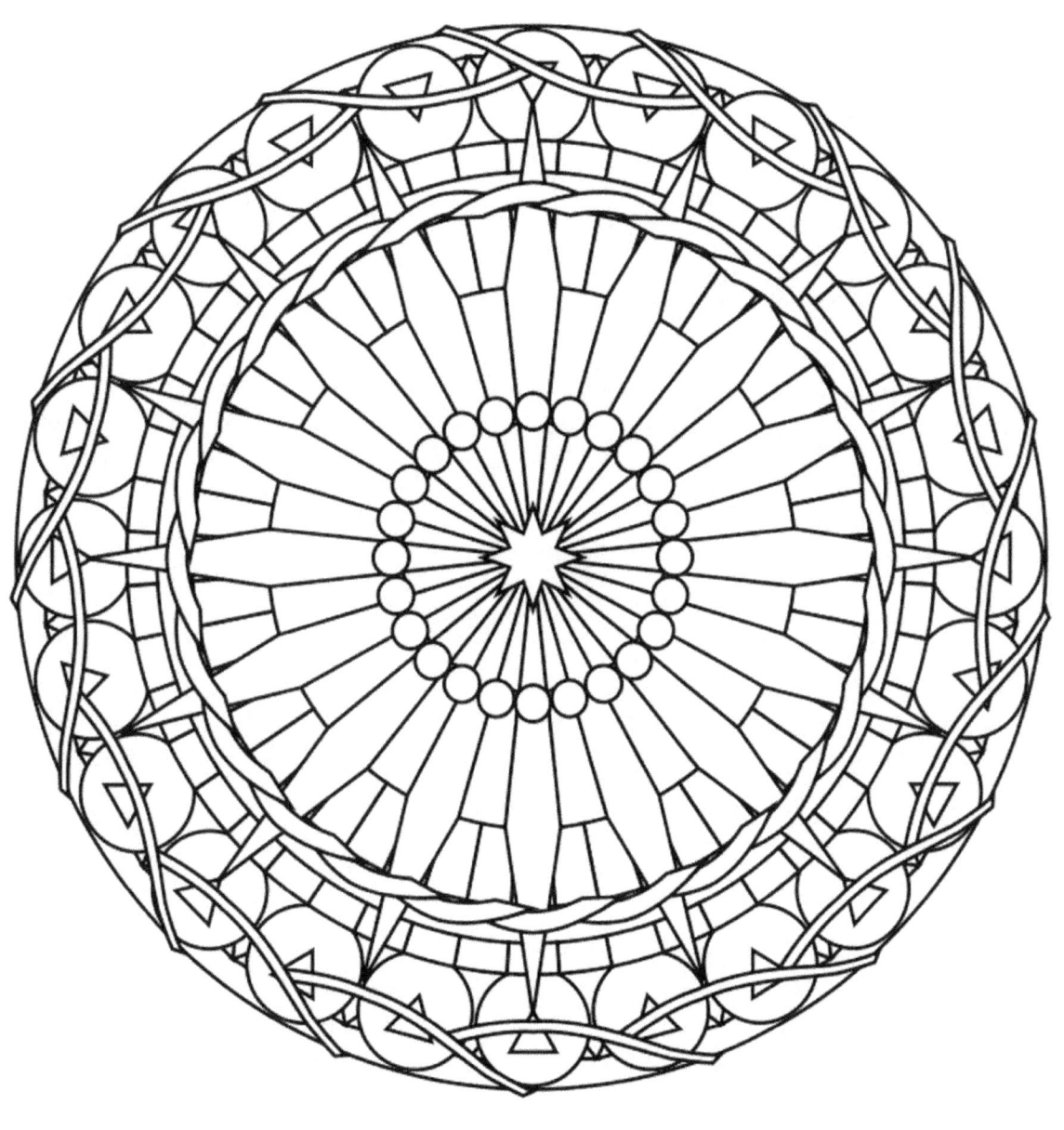

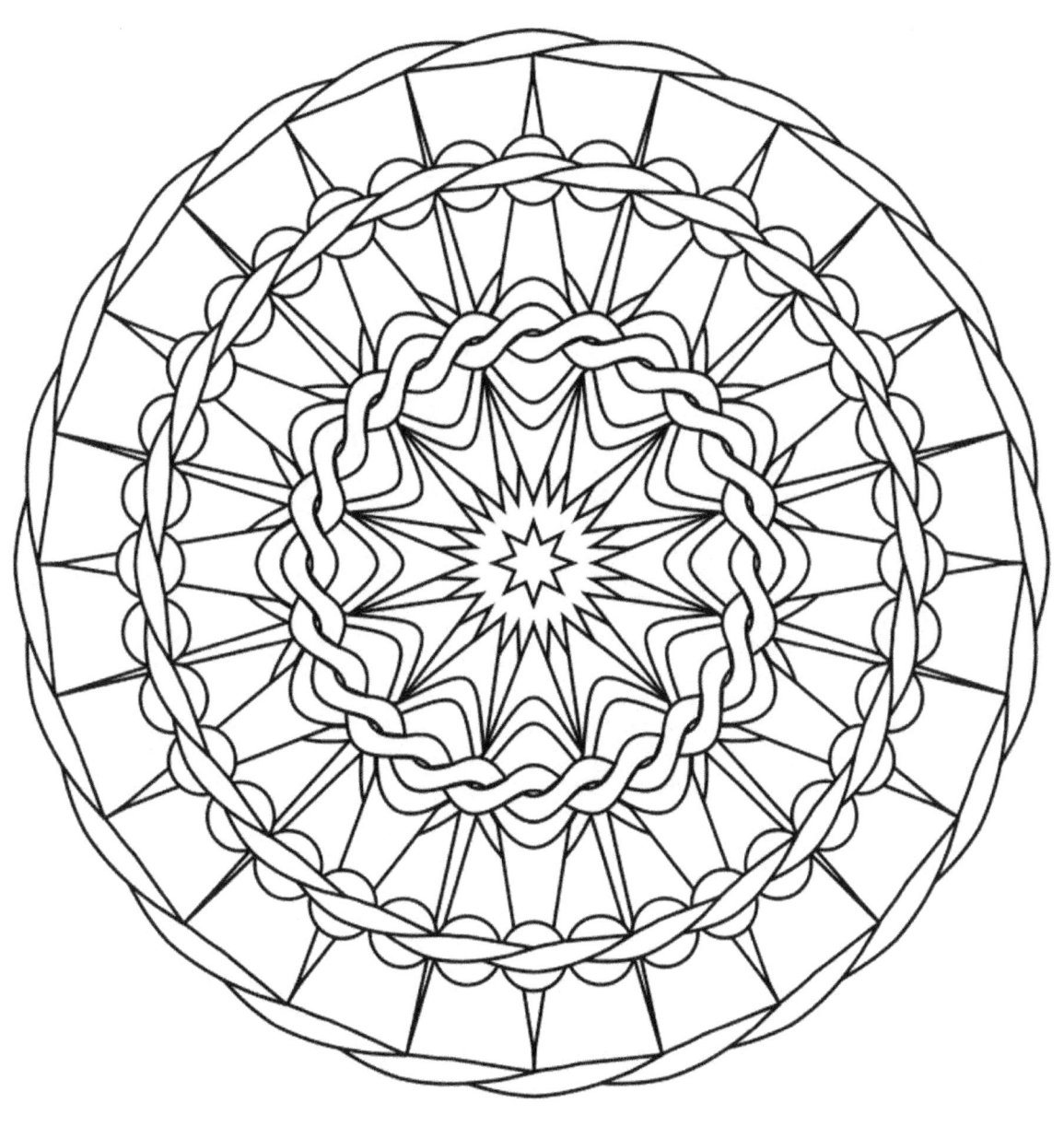

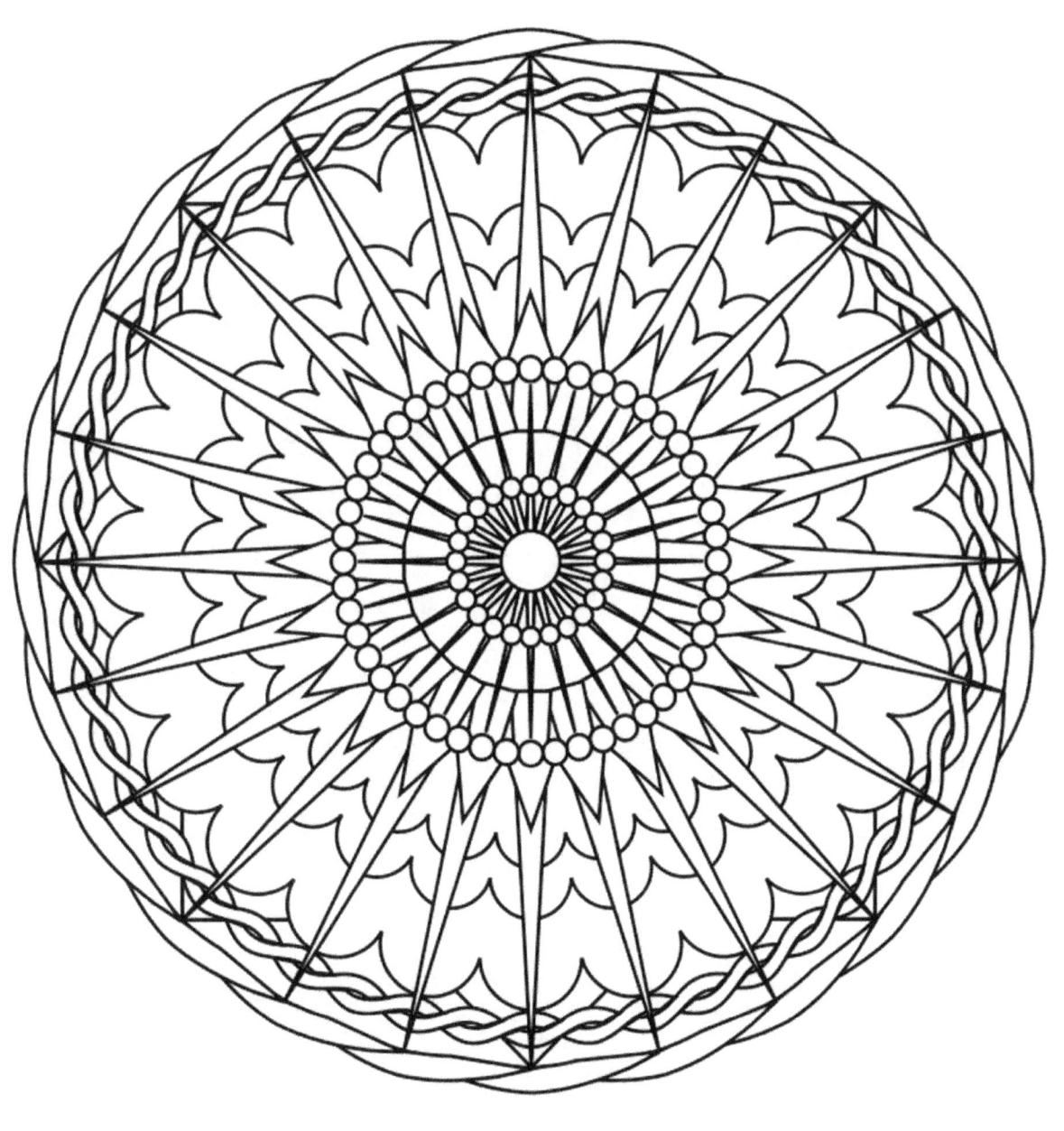

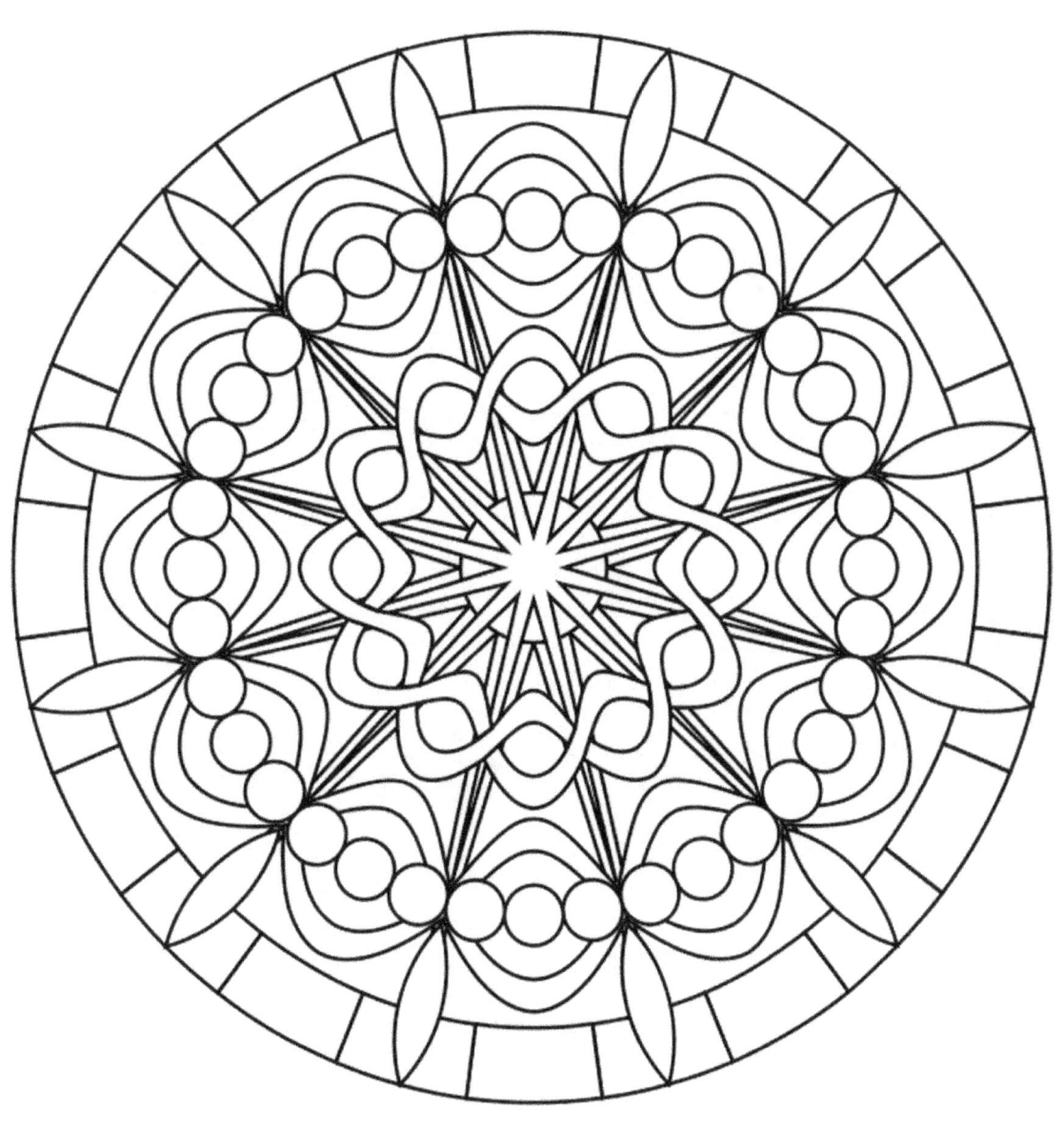

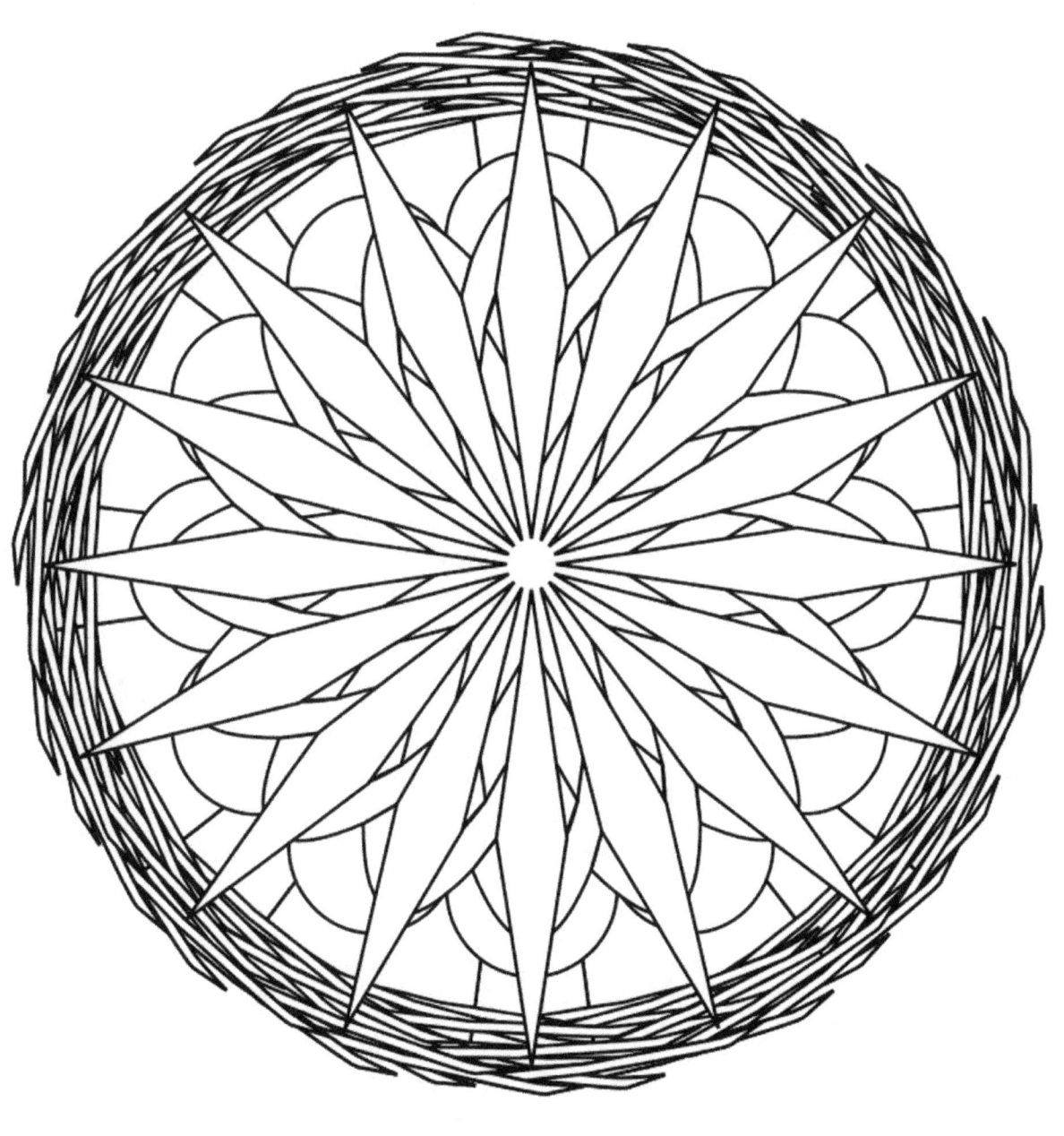

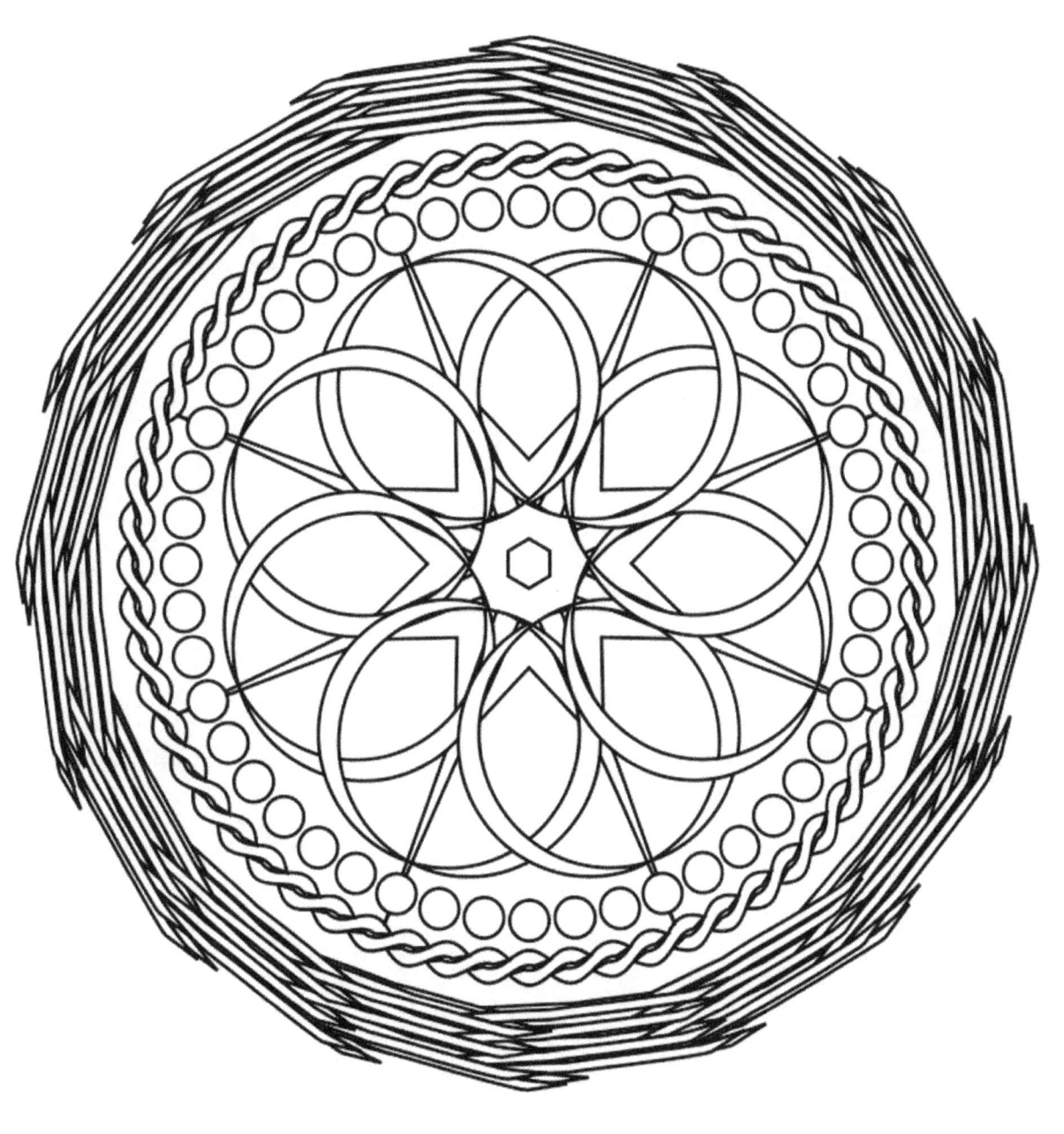

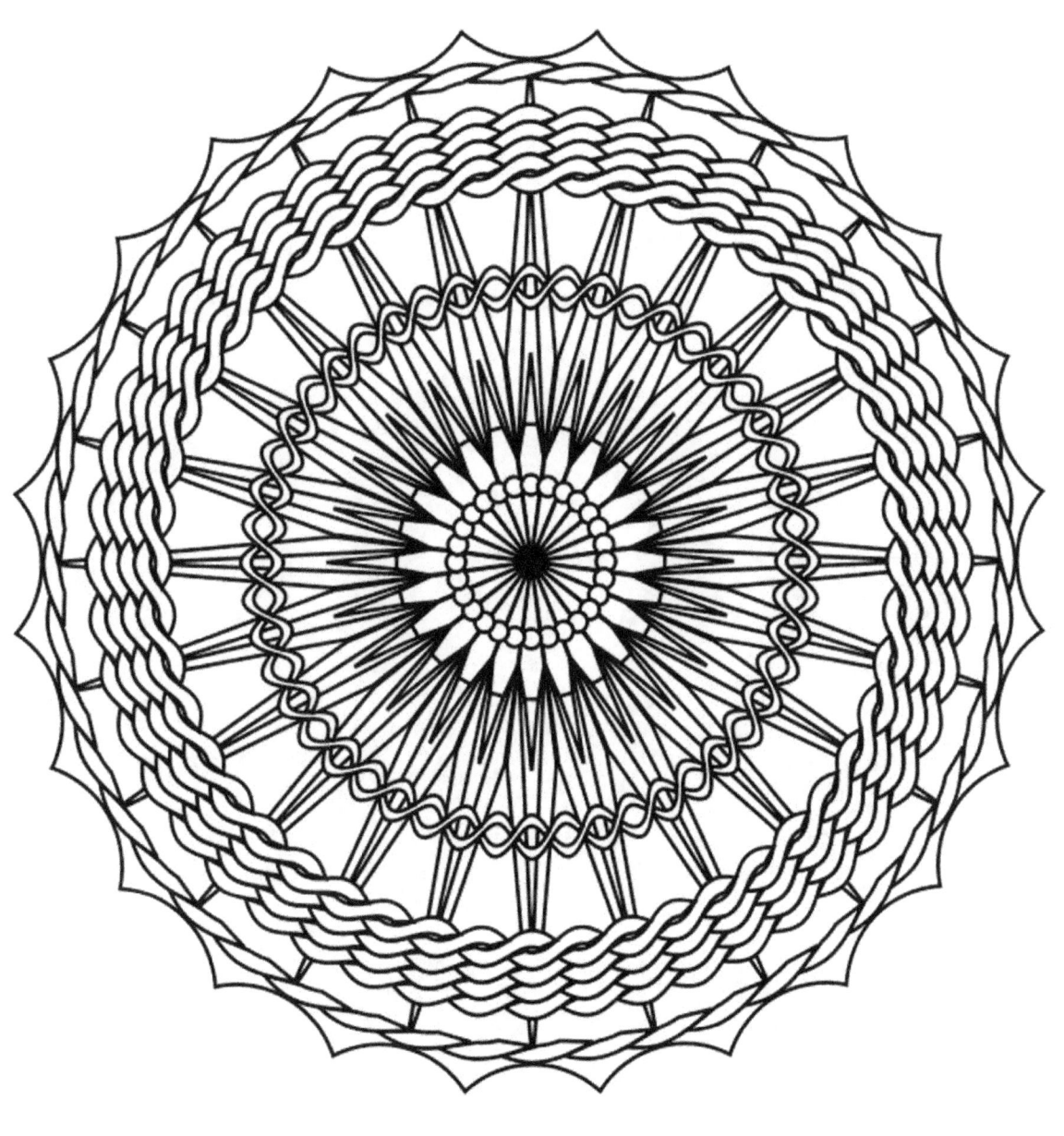

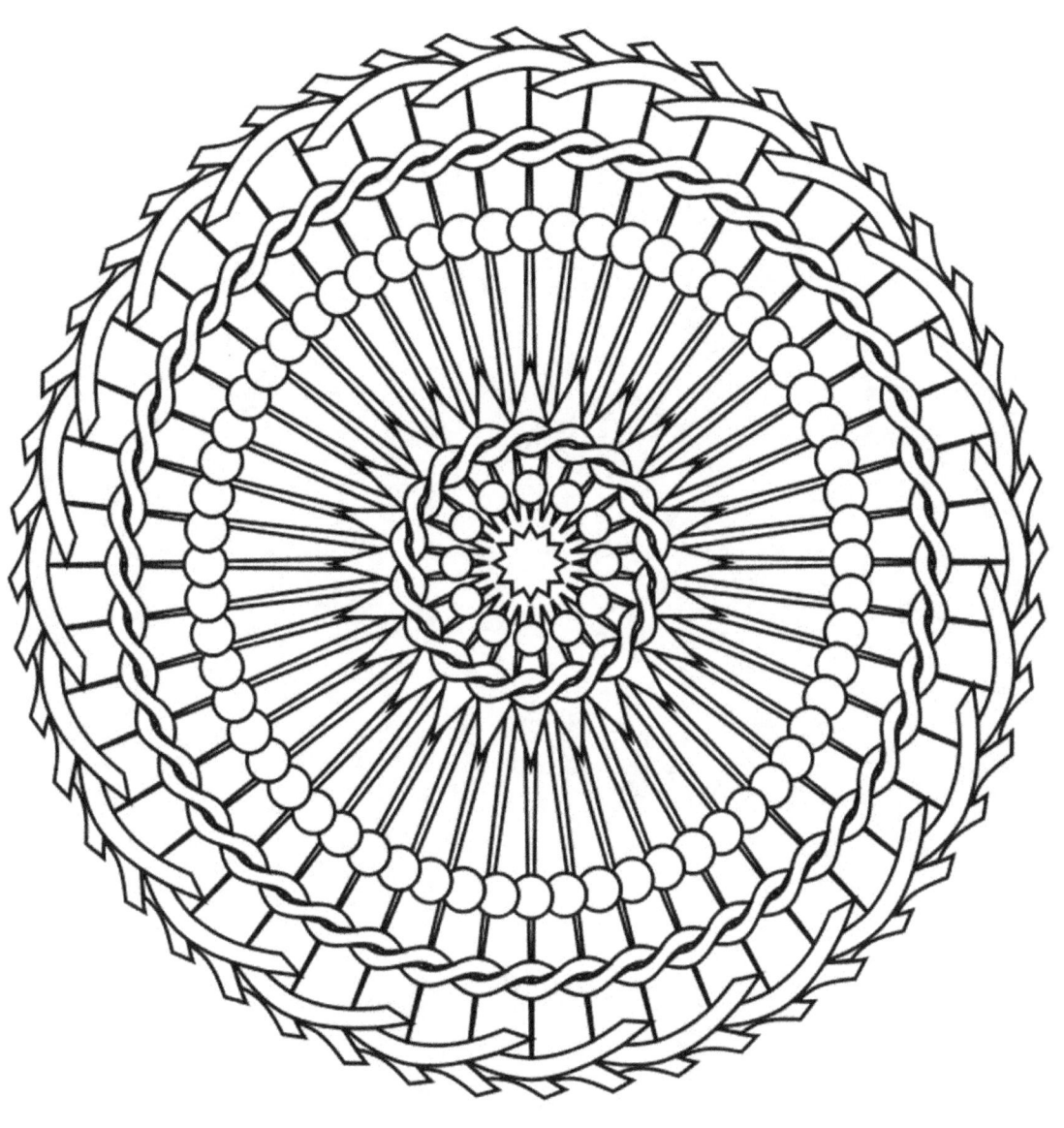

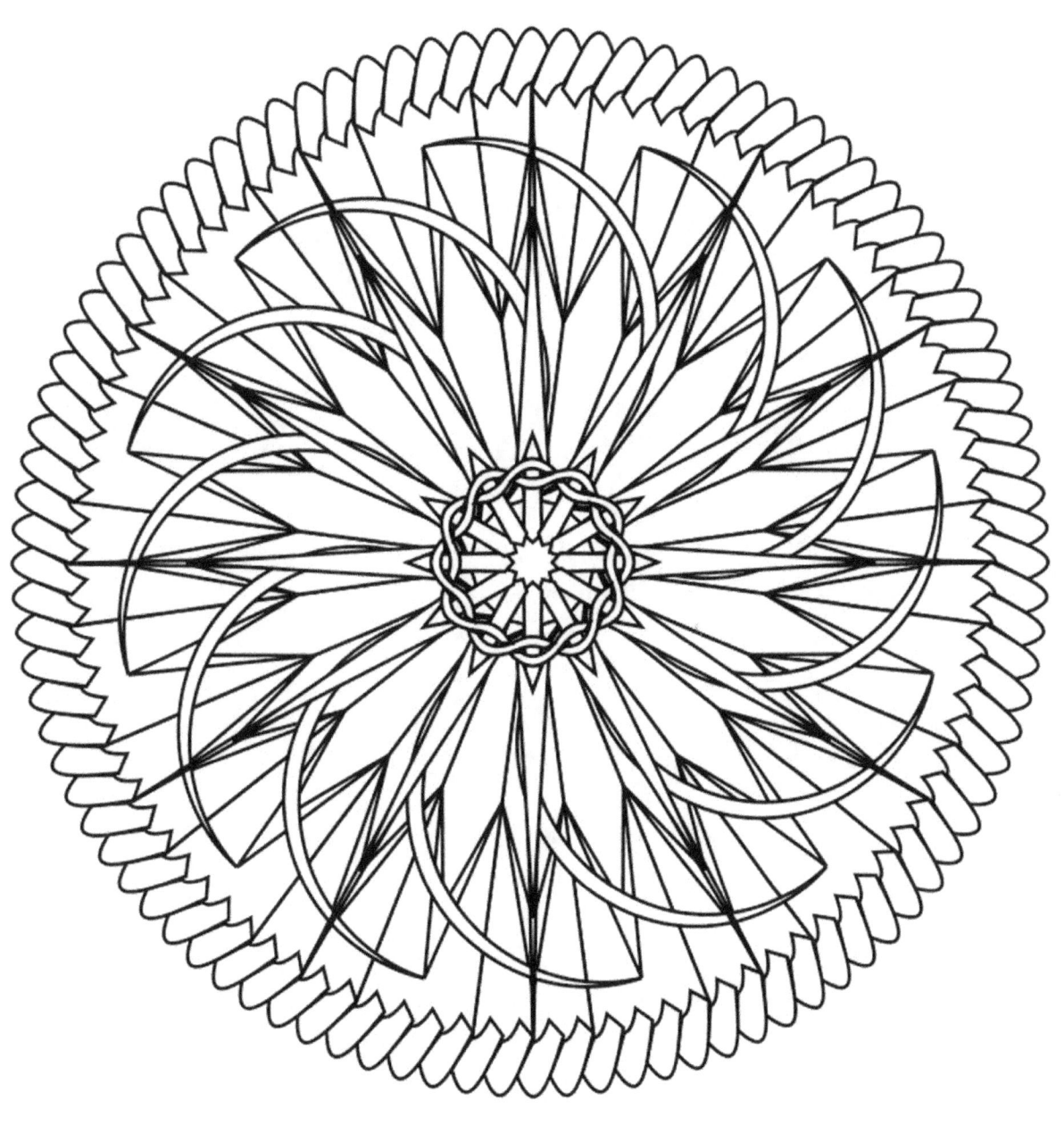

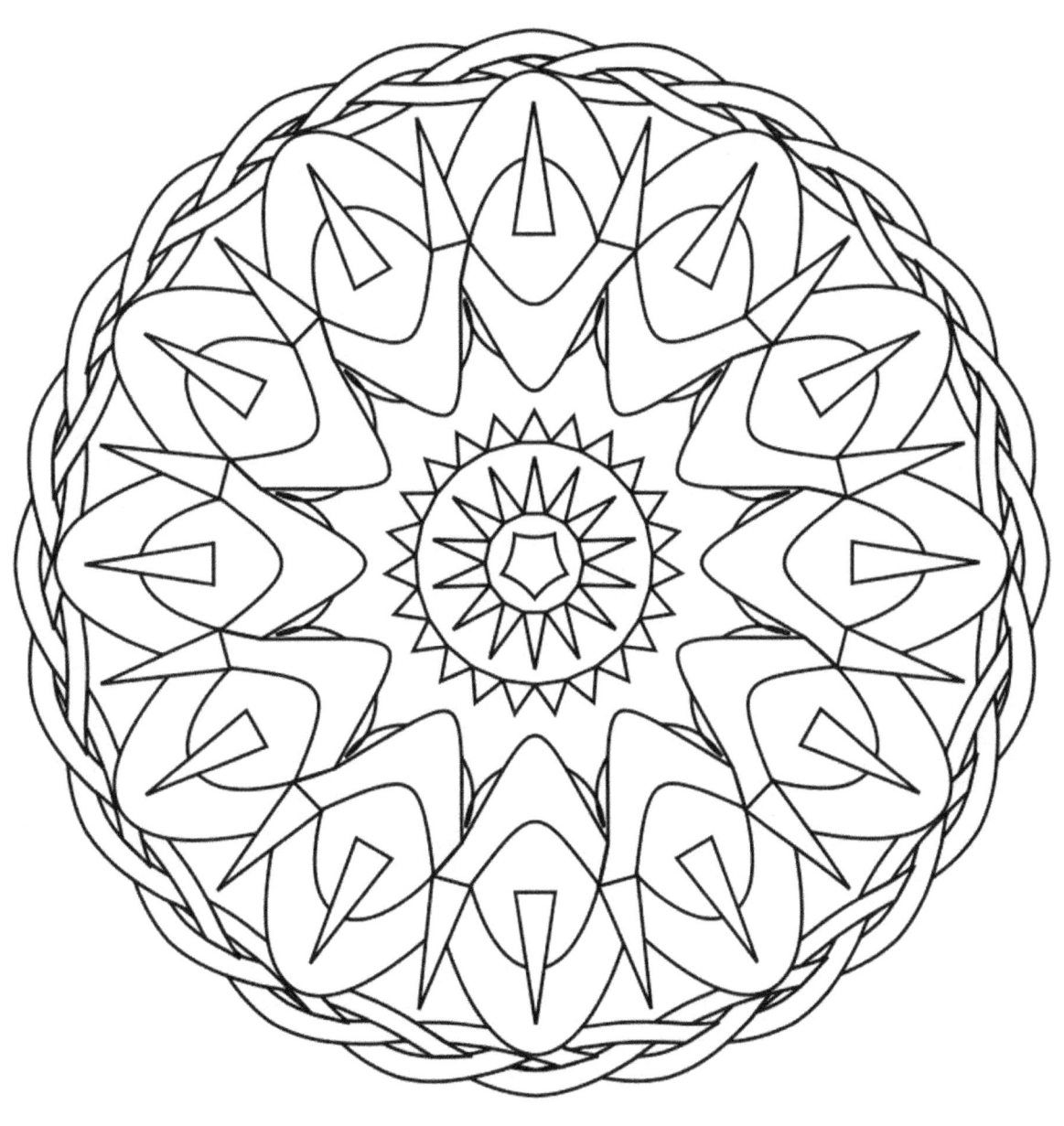

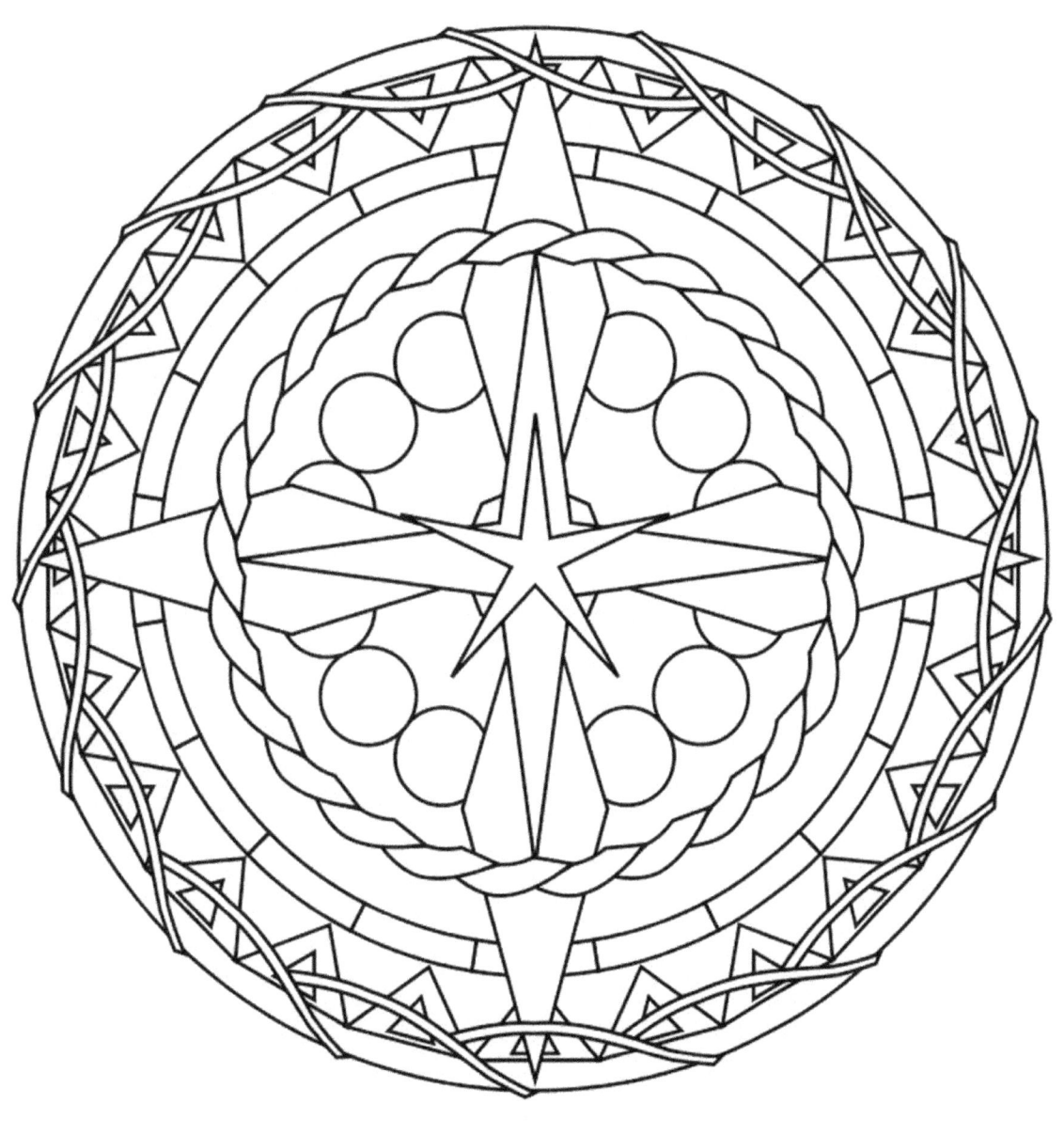

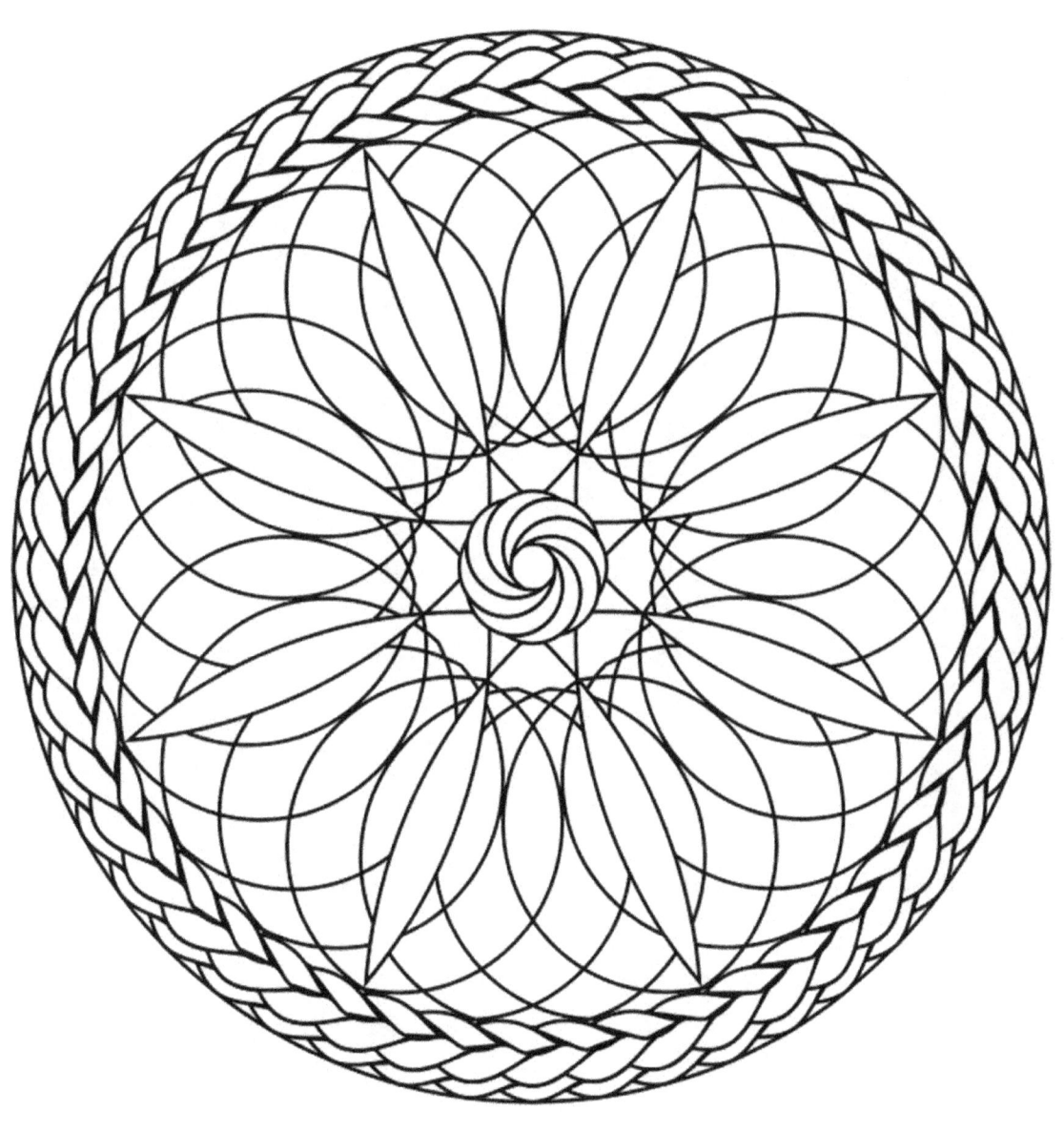

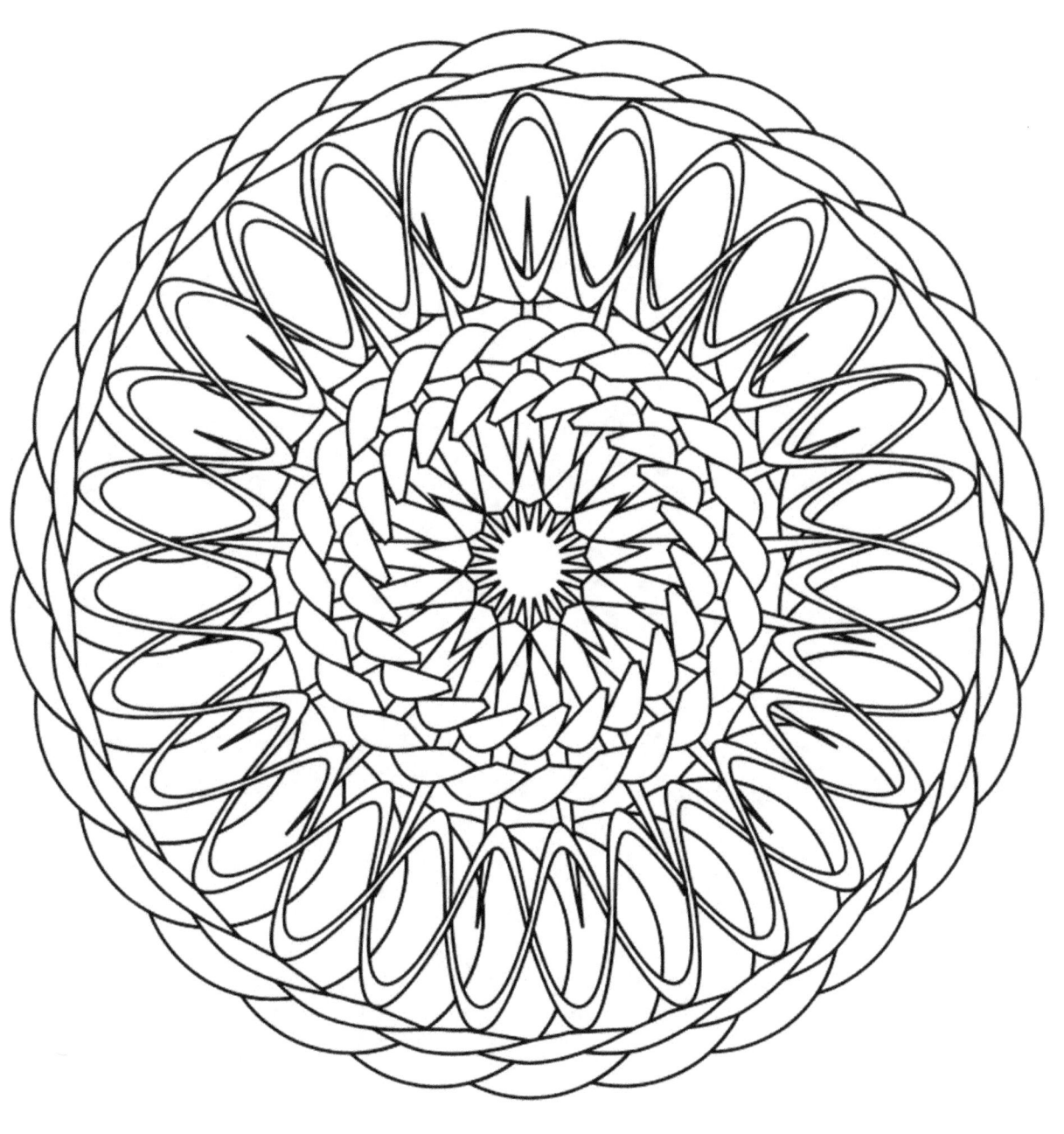

Cosmic Coloring Magic Mandalas - Adult Coloring Books
For direct download PDF (print your own) books.
Please go to : www.azenpublishing.com

For hard copy print books delivered by mail:
Amazon Worldwide - search your local Amazon
for : Cosmic Coloring Magic Mandalas

For Amazon USA:

Cosmic Coloring Magic Mandalas Series 1
http://www.amazon.com/gp/product/1515366251

Cosmic Coloring Magic Mandalas Series 2
http://www.amazon.com/gp/product/1516968158

Cosmic Coloring Magic Mandalas Series3
http://www.amazon.com/gp/product/1517244587

Cosmic Coloring Magic Mandalas Series4
http://www.amazon.com/gp/product/1517135818

For New Zealand (delivery included) hard copy books.

Cosmic Coloring Magic Mandalas Series 1
http://www.fishpond.co.nz/Books/Cosmic-Colouring-Alan-Kiddle/9781515366256

Cosmic Coloring Magic Mandalas Series 2
http://www.fishpond.co.nz/Books/Cosmic-Coloring-Adult-Coloring-Book-Alan-Kiddle/9781516968152

Cosmic Coloring Magic Mandalas Series 3
http://www.fishpond.co.nz/Books/Cosmic-Coloring-Adult-Coloring-Book-Alan-Kiddle/9781517135812

Thank you for purchasing this book.

Are you on Facebook or other social media??
Sharing my images is fine so long as credit is given to the author.
Here's a fun way to do it.
When sharing your coloring just tag me as " Artist - Alan Kiddle "
I will then add you to my artist album and tag you back.
I can't wait to see what you do :-)

Don't forget to join our friendly fun facebook group:
https://www.facebook.com/groups/cosmicmandalas/

If you haven't already joined our publishing journey this is your invitation!
http://azenpublishing.com/index.php/join-us/

Why should you join us ?
    # Have your say in the books we create
    # You will be heard :-)
    # Early bird updates
    # Early bird book sample opportunity's
    # Chances for advance review copy's of new releases
    # We won't bombard you with emails
    # We like to have fun here
    # You can unsubscribe easily at anytime
    # Many fun books in the pipeline
  Questions? Email: cosmicmandalas@gmail.com
Have fun!